U. A. Fan

HOMING IN: SELECTED LOCAL POEMS

Garden Shed

HOMING IN: SELECTED LOCAL POEMS

U. A. Fanthorpe

With original illustrations by R. V. Bailey

THE CYDER PRESS
Cheltenham, England

Acknowledgements

The Cyder Press would like to acknowledge its profound gratitude to
U. A. Fanthorpe, an Honorary Fellow of the University of Gloucestershire,
for allowing it to reprint her own selection of poems about
Gloucestershire and its environs, and to Dr R. V. Bailey for producing
the ten original oil-paintings from which the illustrations to the poems
in this volume have been made. The University and the Press are also
indebted to the Summerfield Trust for a generous grant to assist with
the production of the volume.

This edition first published by The Cyder Press, 2006

ISBN 1 86174 1 174X

Published and produced by the University of Gloucestershire, 2006.

CONTENTS

LIST OF ILLUSTRATIONS

INTRODUCTION:
'Homing In'

U. A. Fanthorpe is not a native of Gloucestershire. She was born in Kent, educated in Surrey and at Oxford, and then she made a break for it and came to live and work in Cheltenham. After sixteen years, a change seemed necessary, and she went to that other country, Wales, for a couple of years. The poetry perhaps really began in Wales - with homesickness. Though we made some good friends and loved the country, like many other writers, the experience of being a foreigner (even in so minimal a sense) was a spur to writing. 'Earthed' – which concludes the present volume - is a poem of joy when she got back to England, to Gloucestershire, to Wotton-under-Edge, where she has lived happily ever after. But safely back in Gloucestershire, there was another experience of foreignness: not this time in another country, but in a job, for she was now working as a receptionist in a Bristol neuro-psychiatric hospital. The strangeness of the patients - and come to that, of the doctors - gave much to think about and write about. This was a most exciting and productive period of writing: every day seemed to bring its own new poem. Driving home, we'd stop under street-lights so that the newest line could be added before it was lost.

The first poems written in the hospital were about the patients, and 'Patients' is typical.[*] We're all 'patients', of course. But some are easier to deal with than others, because – unlike us – they've been labelled. A nine-to-five job (and a job that was inevitably in many ways depressing) provided the spur to get out and about and explore the landscape as much as possible. The nearest new place was of course Bristol, and an early public commission was to write

---

[*]   The ordering of the poems in the present volume follows that of this introductory essay, with the exception of the title-poem, 'Homing In", which opens the selection, and 'Earthed' (see above), which closes it.

poems for a celebration of Bristol. This involved the collaboration of three artists: the musician, Nigel Dodd; the painter, Frank Shipsides; and U. A. as poet. One of her sequence of five poems was 'Friends' Meeting House, Frenchay, Bristol', since Bristol has a fine history of Quaker work. *The Bristol Tryptich*, as the commission was known, was launched at the headquarters of a local building society; this interesting occasion inspired the rather touchy poem 'Reception in Bristol'. 'The West Front at Bath', another poem from those early days, on the other hand, is surely a mediaeval joke - why should angels, fully equipped with wings, need to climb so laboriously up those ladders? And straying slightly further into Somerset, it was the column headed 'Remarks' in the Visitors' Book in Montacute church that provided the title (and other details) for 'Soothing and Awful'.

Already used to Gloucestershire's northern parts - the small-scale grandeur of Tewkesbury, Stow, and so on - there was new local countryside to discover: the more intimate landscapes of the Stroud valleys, the Cirencester area, the edges of Wiltshire. And the kind of energy that went into the exploration of this half-known country spilled over into poetry, too. 'Owlpen Manor', in its lovely setting between Ozleworth and Nympsfield, is itself speaking in the poem: of Margaret of Anjou, wife of Henry VI, and of Tewkesbury, the battle in which her promising only son was killed. As well as her neighbouring counties, Somerset and Wiltshire, Gloucestershire offers much to someone whose historical perspectives are so strongly English: 'Stanton Drew' 'dismantles' the landscape, taking us back through centuries of accretion; 'The Quiet Grave', in honour of almost-lost folk-song, notes the fragility of such life-enhancing links with our past. And there were the special present joys of local ceremonies, like 'Horticultural Show', where the almost sinister beauty of the vegetables is so strikingly different from their humbler cousins in vegetable shops. The little 'redundant' church in our neighbouring village, 'St. James, Charfield', has a memorial to two mysterious unidentified (and unclaimed) children's bodies, found after the famous Charfield railway accident. Details of the unremarked specialness of ordinary days ('May the 8th: how to recognize it') and of the turning year ('Rural Guerrillas') belong very much in the local landscape; 'Neighbours' and 'Elegy for a Cat' celebrate some of the birds and animals who have shared our garden - and our lives.

There were special people, as well, to be celebrated. In Wotton, people are taken really seriously only if they (and preferably their parents) were born here. One of this distinguished group was Amy Cook. She was a striking example of a clever woman who never had the chance to be famous anywhere else, but was famous in Wotton for her wisdom, her staying power, her glorious Gloucestershire accent. We felt honoured by her friendship (as witnessed by the three poems included here). At her funeral, the big parish church was full, and the Silver Band played her out. 'Local Poet' was another well-known Wotton figure, who turned up one evening to ask for advice on which poems he should enter for a poetry competition. Pat, of 'Pat at Milking Time', wasn't local. She was a friend who had emigrated from Shropshire to the edges of Gloucestershire. She was running out of money, and though her goats clearly adored her, she couldn't keep them as they should have been kept. The poem doesn't mention the fearful stink of billy-goat, nor the fact that it needed considerable courage to drink Pat's tea. We hardly knew the extremely old lady of '95'. She lived at the very top of a house in Long Street; the poem imagines what she saw from her third-floor window and how she spent her time, on the edge of her life, and on the edge of the life of the town below.

Old place-names linger in Gloucestershire: 'Strong Language in South Gloucestershire' is a meditation on this; 'On Buying OS Sheet 163' - a map of the environs of Cirencester - indicates how much U. A. likes maps. It offers, as maps do, the pleasures of enjoying a landscape without the effort of walking all over it. 'For OS 759934: 14.2.96. A Love-poem' is a map reference, and it has baffled some people. But it's simply a love-poem to Wotton, the town U. A. lost her heart to from the moment we moved here in 1975. 'Every

Valentine's Day', she says, 'I feel like plastering this poem all over Wotton's telegraph poles and notice boards' (this hasn't happened yet, but it still may). 'Wotton Walks', an introduction to all the possible walks into and out of the town, is really another such love-poem, though its origin was in the days when U.A. was, briefly, a Cotswold Way Warden. One of the walks takes you through the little Conygre Wood, very near where we live. In the springtime it's full of wood-anemones, and then garlic and bluebells. The early botanists wanted the English bluebell to be a relation of the Greek hyacinth, but our local bluebells are illiterate: they haven't the special letters *ai ai* that Greek hyacinths have. But there's much to be said, nevertheless, for these silent bluebells of England, and U.A. speaks up for them in 'Conygre Wood and Hyakinthoides Non-Scriptus'.

Just over the hill from Wotton lies North Nibley, the birthplace of William Tyndale, the great Bible translator. As you travel along the M5 you can see his monument on the hill. Tyndale spent some time as a tutor in Gloucestershire, but for much of his life he was on the run, pursued by powerful churchmen furious at his translating the scriptures into English. Eventually he was imprisoned in Vilvorde Castle; then, in 1536, strangled and burnt at the stake. The sequence, 'Tyndale in Darkness', imagines him during a week in that prison, without light or warmth, remembering the Cotswolds and the sights he could see, on the Severn, from the hill over North Nibley. The poem was unofficially 'commissioned' when our Vicar mentioned that he'd welcome a change, one Easter, from Stainer's *Crucifixion* - and U.A. took up the challenge.

For two happy years in the 1980s, U.A. was Arts Council Writer-in-Residence at St. Martin's College in Lancaster, and so became very familiar with the M5 and M6, the quickest route home, and with all the watersheds, landmarks and place-names on the way, as well as the curious superstitions such an often-repeated journey develops. The title-poem, 'Homing In', catalogues these moments. After that there was little time for local pursuits. The hospital job claimed her for several more years, and increasingly the world of poetry did, too. By the end of the 1980s there were four full collections and a King Penguin *Selected Poems*, and some of the poetry was making its way on to school examination syllabuses - something which U.A. viewed with consternation, having been seriously put off poetry herself during her schooldays. The examination boards don't seem to consult with poets about including their work in this way: indeed, had we not had friends who acted as spies in the teaching profession we'd perhaps never have known about the situation - nor about the fascinating questions that appeared in examination papers. One day we came across a secondhand copy of *Selected Poems*, with the answers, in a schoolboy hand, in the margins. The response considered appropriate to 'set texts' found its way into 'Dear Mr Lee', which was a poem commissioned for a Cheltenham celebration in honour of the famous Gloucestershire writer, Laurie Lee, and the imagined 'set text' is his *Cider with Rosie*. U.A. says she is herself the model for Mr Smart, the repressive English teacher in the poem, though those who were taught by her will know very well where her sympathies really lie.

Of the other Cheltenham poems, 'Carol Concert' and 'Staff Party' spring from teaching days, the first about the annual Christmas concert at the Ladies' College, where recent school-leavers show off what they really look like to those still in school uniform, their young men brought along as trophies to the occasion. 'Staff Party', on the other hand, deals with the strange ways colleagues know - and don't know - each other, and the even stranger myths about them that grow up among their pupils, whose fervent curiosity reminds one of Suetonius, the gossipy Roman historian who wrote about Nero and Caligula and other colourful characters. In 'Last House', the cinema was the one almost opposite the College. It was called The Regal. One day, on a return visit to Cheltenham, we saw the building being demolished, and watching the great destructive ball crashing into it we remembered the old place in its Saturday morning splendour, with all the local children queueing up outside.

'What about Jerusalem?' celebrates the Cheltenham district midwife, Gwen. Loyal, kind, brave, exasperating, she always saw the right thing to do and did it. There were no inhibitions in her friendship.

All her life, U.A. has loved rivers and inland waterways, especially the Thames between London and Oxford. We bought our first boat (a sort of floating soap-dish) impetuously one holiday in Rye in Sussex, and after various courageous encounters with the quieter reaches of the Severn and with the Gloucester and Sharpness Canal, we began to spend time exploring other canals, eventually investing in a much-loved second-hand narrowboat. At about this time, in the mid-1970s, the restoration of the Sapperton Tunnel (an impressive two miles long) was beginning to take place, and the splendid eastern portal of the tunnel, by the Tunnel House Inn at Coates, near Cirencester, was formally unveiled by Lord Bathurst in 1977. The canal was built in the eighteenth century to link the Severn and the Thames, but the tunnelling that was needed was difficult, as it went through limestone, and the excavations were always collapsing. The poem 'Canal 1977' sees the tunnel as it was then (in 1977), and as it had been before, with the leggers (who propelled the boat with their legs, as they lay on their backs on the deck-head, because the horses had to go overland, not through the tunnel), and imagines it as, with luck, it would be when the canal was fully restored. The Welsh 'Roman candle miners', who sat on their barrel of gunpowder as it was lowered through holes into the eighteenth-century workings, often set fire to themselves. Danger is still not far from the waterways of today: from 'Purton Lower Bridge' (opposite the Berkeley Arms) you can see how close to the domestic tranquillity of the Sharpness canal lies the treacherous Severn.

Every year since 1972 U.A. has written a poem for our Christmas card, which we print on our small press. This Christmas poem has always been a bit of a challenge: we hadn't much type when we began, and only very short poems were possible. And the cards had to meet the needs of such a wide range of recipients: young, old, devout, ungodly, the poetically sophisticated as well as the poetically innocent. The cast of Christmas characters - angels, donkey, Virgin, robin, star, etc., were soon used up. So 'The Invitation' (spoken by the Wotton foxes) and 'The Wicked Fairy at the Manger' involve some of the uncanonical newcomers that have made their way into the gospel story over the years.

'The Apple War' had an interesting beginning. It was written at the request of Gloucester Royal Hospital. The hospital had been obliged to fell an orchard in order to make room for a maternity wing, and to keep faith with the past it very properly decided to plant apple trees at convenient corners on the new site. U.A. was intrigued to be the person behind the shiny new spade, digging the first hole for planting: it was quite difficult to get her to understand that only a symbolic dig was required, for the photographer, not a whole afternoon's work. At least on this occasion the sun shone, and the 'Awkward Subject' wasn't expected to pose on a windswept hill.

Some poets write best when they're on the edge of despair, some when they're solitary in libraries. Except perhaps for the initial explosion of the early hospital poems, ignited as they were by anger at the patients' helplessness, a rooted happiness has always been the most promising seed-bed for U.A.'s poems, even for the darkest and most searching. The poems began in the early 1970s, just as we began to live in Wotton, and this undistinguished very special Gloucestershire town has proved such a nourishing place that there's never been the slightest need to move on anywhere else. Asked once at a reading which was her favourite journey, U.A. unhesitatingly replied 'Home - from anywhere!'

R.V. Bailey
Wotton-under-Edge

Homing In

Homing In

Somewhere overseas England are struggling
On a sticky wicket; somewhere in Europe
An elder statesman is dying *adagio*; and here,
Nowhere precisely, I slip to pips and bens
Through the occupied air.

Somewhere along this road an invisible ditch
Signals tribe's end, an important mutation of [ʌ];
Somewhere among these implacable place-names
People are living coherent lives. For me the unfocussed
Landscape of exile.

Somewhere along this watershed weather
Will assert itself, swap wet for dry,
Scribble or flare on windscreens, send freak gusts
Sneaking round juggernauts, ravel traffic with
A long foggy finger.

Home starts at Birmingham. Places
Where I have walked are my auguries:
The stagey Malverns, watery sharp Bredon,
May Hill's arboreal quiff. These as I pass
Will bring me luck if they look my way.

I should be rehearsing contingencies,
Making resolutions, allowing for change
In the tricky minor modes of love. But,
Absorbed by nearly-home names,
Dear absurd Saul, Framilode, Frampton-on-Severn,

I drop, unprepared, into one particular
Parish, one street, one house, one you,
Exact, ignorant and faithful as swallows commuting
From Sahara to garage shelf.

Patients

Not the official ones, who have been
Diagnosed and made tidy. They are
The better sort of patient.

They know the answers to the difficult
Questions on the admission sheet
About religion, next of kin, sex.

They know the rules. The printed ones
In the *Guide for Patients*, about why we prefer
No smoking, the correct postal address;

Also the real ones, like the precise quota
Of servility each doctor expects,
When to have fits, and where to die.

These are not true patients. They know
Their way around, they present the right
Symptoms. But what can be done for us,

The undiagnosed? What drugs
Will help our Matron, whose cats are
Her old black husband and her young black son?

Who will prescribe for our nurses, fatally
Addicted to idleness and tea? What therapy
Will relieve our Psychiatrist of his lust

For young slim girls, who prudently
Pretend to his excitement, though age
Has freckled his hands and his breath smells old?

How to comfort our Director through his
Terminal distress, as he babbles of
Football and virility, trembling in sunlight?

There is no cure for us. O, if only
We could cherish our bizarre behaviour
With accurate clinical pity. But there are no

Notes to chart our journey, no one
Has even stamped CONFIDENTIAL or *Not to be
Taken out of the hospital* on our lives.

Friends' Meeting House, Frenchay, Bristol

When the doors of the house are shut,
Eyes lidded, mouth closed, nose and ears
Doing their best to idle, fingers allowed out
Only on parole; when the lovely holy distractions,
Safe scaffolding of much-loved formulae,
Have been rubbed away; then the plant
Begins to grow. It is hard to rear,
Rare herb of silence, through which the Word comes.
Three centuries of reticent, meticulous lives
Have naturalised it on this ground.

And the herb is the Vine, savage marauder,
That spreads and climbs unstoppably,
Filling the house, the people, with massing insistent shoots
That leaf through windows and doors, that rocket through
                                   chimneys,
Till flesh melts into walking forms of green,
Trained to the wildness of Vine, which exacts
Such difficult witness; whose work is done
In hopeless places, prisons, workhouses,
In countinghouses of respectable merchants,
In barracks, collieries, sweatshops, in hovels
Of driven and desperate men.

                            It begins here
In the ground of silence.

Reception in Bristol

These men are rich; they buy
Pictures before asking prices.

Their shirts are exquisite; I know instinctively
I must not say so.

Conversations are precisely timed,
Costing so much per word per minute.

Wives are worn small this year, soberly dressed.
Their eyes are wild, but there is no exit.

Schools that encourage music, says the chairman,
Have no hooligans. No one replies.

The photographer is our memento mori.
He takes two sandwiches at once

From the curtseying waitress. There is a crumb
At the corner of his mouth, and he has

To go on somewhere else. He is here to remind us
That in this city Savage died, a prisoner;

That Chatterton poisoned himself in his London garret
Rather than creep back here.

The West Front at Bath

The headscarfed tourists in the comfy shoes
Obediently make their scheduled pause
Among the pigeons. Sun and stone confuse
The rhythm of their uninformed applause.
Where are we now? Would it be Bath, perhaps?
Five o'clock deftly shoots its slanted gleam
Across their eyes. A thoughtless pigeon claps
His wings. This moment is as much a dream
As Jacob's nightmare on the Abbey wall,
Alive with straining angels, who with wing
Correctly folded, desperately crawl
Along their monstrous ladder. Evening
Distorts their poise. Above it all sits God,
Watching the dreams, and finding both kinds odd.

'Soothing and Awful'

(Visitors' Book at Montacute church)

You are meant to exclaim. The church
Expects it of you. Bedding plants
And polished brass anticipate a word.

Visitors jot a name,
A nationality, briskly enough,
But find *Remarks* beyond them.

I love English churches!
Says Friedrichshafen expansively.
The English are more backward. They come,

Certainly, from Spalding, Westbury-on-Trym,
The Isle of Wight; but all the words
They know are: *Very Lovely; Very Peaceful; Nice*.

A giggling gaggle from Torquay Grammar,
All pretending they can't spell *beautiful*, concoct
A private joke about the invisible organ.

A civilized voice from Cambridge
Especially noticed the well-kept churchyard.
Someone from Dudley, whose writing suggests tight shoes,

Reported *Nice and Cool*. The young entry
Yelp their staccato approval:
Super! Fantastic! Jesus Lives! Ace!

But what they found,
Whatever it was, it wasn't what
They say. In the beginning,

We know, the word, but not here,
Land of the perpetually-flowering cliché,
The rigid lip. Our fathers who piled

Stone upon stone, our mothers
Who stitched the hassocks, our cousins
Whose bones lie smooth, harmonious around –

However majestic their gifts, comely their living,
Their words would be thin like ours; they would join
In our inarticulate anthem: *Very Cosy*.

Owlpen Manor

I am folded among my terraces
Like an old dog half asleep.
The sunlight tickles my chimneys.

I have never cared for grandeur.
This narrow handcarved valley fits
My casual autocracy. But I hold

What's mine. The long, undistinguished
Dynasty of Cotswold gentlemen,
Who never married cleverly, and made

Only a modest fortune in Ireland,
Suited my fancy. Owlpens, Daunts
And Stoughtons, I charmed them to a happy

Apathy. Even Margaret, my ghost of Anjou,
Pacing my Great Chamber in her high-crowned hat,
Knowing that tomorrow is Tewkesbury,

Walks in benevolence. My floorboards creak
In their infinite adjustment to time.
I have outlasted my successor on the hill,

I am permanent as the muted roar
Of white pigeons in my barn, as the drift
Of dry leaves in my ancient garden.

Stanton Drew

First you dismantle the landscape.
Take away everything you first
Thought of. Trees must go,
Roads, of course, the church,
Houses, hedges, livestock, a wire
Fence. The river can stay,
But loses its stubby fringe
Of willows. What do you
See now? Grass, the circling
Mendip rim, with its notches
Fresh, like carving. A sky
Like ours, but empty along
Its lower levels. And earth
Stripped of its future, tilted
Into meaning by these stones,
Pitted and unemphatic. Recreate them.
They are the most permanent
Presences here, but cattle, weather,
Archaeologists have rubbed against them.
Still in season they will
Hold the winter sun poised
Over Maes Knoll's white cheek,
Chain the moon's footsteps to
The pattern of their dance.
Stand inside the circle. Put
Your hand on stone. Listen
To the past's long pulse.

The Quiet Grave

(for Cecil Sharp)

Underground Rome waited solidly
In stone patience. Orpheus might lose
A beast or two, cracked apart by roots
Of brambled centuries, but still
Foundations lasted, knowing, like the princess,
That one day a ferret and a boy
Exploring a rabbithole would find an empire.

But this was a kingdom that lived

Some kinds of earth are reliable. The black
Peats of Somerset, and Norfolk mud
That tenderly cradled the deathship's spectral
Longrotted timbers. Some kinds of dryasdust
Air, too, responsibly cherish papyrus.

But this was a kingdom that lived
In the living air

Who held the keys of the kingdom?
Unfriendly old men in workhouses;
Bedridden ninety-year-olds terrorized
By highhanded grandchildren; gipsy women
With the long memories of the illiterate;
Old sailors who could sing only
Within sound of the sea. These
Held the keys of the kingdom.

Where was the kingdom?
The kingdom was everywhere. Under the noses
Of clerics devoted to folklore it lived
Invisibly, in gardens, in fields and kitchens,
In the servants' quarters. No one could find it
But those who were in it already.

When was the kingdom?
The kingdom was while women washed
And men broke stones. It was
Intervals in birdscaring; between
A cup too low and a cup
Too high; when a great-grandfather
Sang like a lark. Then
Was the kingdom.

Who cared for the kingdom?
An old woman gathering stones,
Who seized Sharp by his gentle-
Manly lapels, blowing her song into his mind
Through wrinkled gums. A surly chap
In Bridgewater Union, holding
Sharp's hand between his own grim bones,
Tears falling on all three. These
Cared for the kingdom.

What were the treasures of the kingdom?
Scraps of other worlds, prized
For their strangeness. A derrydown and a heyho,
And a rue dum day and a fol the diddle dee.
These were the treasures of the kingdom.

Who were the heirs of the kingdom?
The kingdom had no heirs, only
A younger generation that winked
At senility's music, and switched on the gramophone.

What was the end of the kingdom?
Massed choirs of the Federation
Of Women's Institutes filling
The Albert Hall; laconic
Improper poetry improved
For the benefit of schools;
Expansion of the Folk Song Industry. These
Were the end of the kingdom.

For this was a kingdom that lived
In the dying air

Horticultural Show

These are Persephone's fruits
Of the underyear. These will guide us
Through the slow dream of winter.

Onions her paleskinned lamps.
Rub them for strange knowledge. They shine
With the light of the tomb.

Drawn in fine runes along
Hard green rinds, the incomprehensible
Initiation of the marrow.

All orange energy driven
Down to a final hair, these carrots
Have been at the heart of darkness.

And parti-coloured leeks,
Their green hair plaited, like Iroquois braves,
Leaning exhausted in corners.

Holystoned the presence
Of potatoes, pure white and stained pink.
Persephone's bread.

Sacrificed beetroots
Display their bleeding hearts. We read
The future in these entrails.

Out in the world excitable
Ponies caper, Punch batters Judy, a man
Creates a drystone wall in thirty minutes,

Arrows fly, coconuts fall, crocodiles
And Jubilee mugs, disguised as children,
Cope with candyfloss, the band
Adds its slow waltz heart beat.

Here in the tent, in the sepia hush,
Persephone's fruits utter where they have been,
Where we are going.

St. James's, Charfield

(a redundant church)

Someone has left riddles here,
Relic of the interrogative mode
Licensed to be used in churches.

The seven signs of Charfield:

A *bier*, since all flesh is,
And churchyards are never redundant,
Dying remaining the most
Favoured single activity.

A *sparrow*, claws up, for the fallen,
And to remind us how many we are worth.

A *Bible*, revised but sinister:
He also suppressed the hill-shrines
And the sacred poles in Judah.
Jehoshaphat, professing urban religion.

An *organ*, midget, defunct,
Which roared *Aargh* like a maniac
Being touched.

Emptiness, left behind by pews,
Vestments, guidebooks, kneelers,
The gaudy clutter of mortality. What stays
Is anybody's guess. It flutters,
And is full of light.

Pinned to the door, a *list*
Of the churchyard's flora: *I do hope*
That you will be able to manage
This interesting site in the best way
For the wildlife. And names,
Instead of the flower-arrangers, the flowers:
Cow-parsley, columbine, cuckoo-pint, daisy.

Last, the *memorial*,
In discreet granite memory
Of *those who lost their lives*
In the railway accident at Charfield:
Persons from Belper, Milverton,
Gloucester, Sheffield; couples
From Leicester, Derby, Plymouth;
Two children, never identified,
The hairs of whose heads someone
Omitted to number.

Please,
No weedkiller to be used in the churchyard.

Dandelion time

May 8th: how to recognize it

The tulips have finished their showy conversation.
Night's officers came briefly to report,
And took their heads off.

The limes have the look of someone
Who has been silent a long time,
And is about to say a very good thing.

Roses grow taller, leafier,
Duller. They have star parts;
Like great actors, they hang about humbly in the wings.

On the lawn, daisies sustain their candid
Childish shout. Hippy dandelions are stoned
Out of their golden minds. And always

The rub-a-dub-dub recapitulation
Of grass blades growing. The plum tree is resting
Between blossom and fruit. Like a poker-player,

She doesn't show her hand. Daffodils
Are a matter of graceless brown leaves and rubber bands.
Wallflowers have turned bony.

This is not the shining childhood of spring,
But its homely adolescence, angular, hypothetical.
How one regrets the blue fingertips staggering
Up from the still dank earth.

On Wotton Hill

Rural Guerrillas

The dead sticks of winter rise in their graves.
The future pokes through them, exploding
Like pointillist grapeshot.

Landroving weeds lay jagged boobytraps.
Young daffodils rear ponderous heads
The shape of torpedoes.

Along the hedgerows impatient snipers
Pepper the air with their random bright
Volleys, declaring green.

The shouts and stutters and shamefaced mumbles
Of garden birds: recruits rehearsing
The trenches' foul language.

In the air, incorrigible Cockney
Thumbs-up of chestnut buds, embarking
For the spring offensive.

Under the tarmac the depth charge daisies
Brace knees and shoulders for the moment
When they hijack the world.

Neighbours

The Collared couple lived at number one,
In the guttering. They were good neighbours,
Kept an orderly house, the missus was always home.
They might have been R.C. Her tender nape
Bent over her brood was slightly Madonna-ish,
And the three notes they chanted all day, all day,
Some kind of psalm?

Ivy made the gable a high-rise ghetto;
The Blackies at 1b were a racketty lot.
Kept odd hours, zoomed home like motorbikes revving,
Tried to mug the Collareds, at the least excuse
Would scream blue murder, threaten to call the cops.
It was because of them the cat left home.

Our next-door neighbours keep themselves to themselves.
We swap small talk and seedlings over the fence
Sometimes but not too often. You have to keep
A certain distance.

Two terrorists at large in our neighbourhood
Must have holed up somewhere close. We haven't seen them.
Our neighbours have. *Her*, with her kill,
Standing as if at home on the compost heap,
One foot upraised to pluck. She didn't move,
Outstared them till they backed into the house.
They talk of her yellow eyes, her butcher's poise,
The pigeon bleeding in her taloned fist.

To be a sparrowhawk's neighbour is an honour,
And yet the harmless squabs and fledgling blacks
(Her prey) are neighbours too. We let them be,
And then she guts them for the fluffy brood
She nurtures with the aweswome tenderness
We see on television.

                We don't say this
To our human neighbours, not-quite-friends,
In case they think we're soft. You have to keep
A certain distance.

Elegy for a Cat

'Cats being the least moveable of animals because of their strong local
predilections; they are indeed in a domesticated state the serfs of the
animal creation, and properly attached to the soil.'
(Southey: *Memoir of the Cats of Greta Hall*)

Yours was the needlework, precise and painful
As claws on a loved naked shoulder, that sewed us
Back into that Merthyr morning, when, terrorised by toddlers,
You mined under our alien gateway, claimed sanctuary
In a jacket pocket.

You were the first to join our outlandish outfit
On that hilltop housing estate, with the garage-in-name-only,
Invisible agog neighbours, rhubarb corms from Aberfan;
You the first source of our logged jokes, with
Your ears akimbo,

Eyes so excited they retreated behind their withers,
Living a paw-to-mouth existence, elbowing your way
Up bodies like a midshipman up rigging
Your whiskers wet with passion, sitting with one ear
In a human mouth, to keep warm.

I was never sure that English was your language,
Though you were probably just as dim in Welsh,
Vague about status, doglike coming to a whistle,
Running on white bandy-legs with a
Welcoming cluck.

You never took offence, were always ready
With an Eskimo kiss of your pink plebeian nose;
Set records for slow learning when we installed
The cat-flap; had no idea of the gravitas
Proper to cats.

Exiled in Gloucestershire, you domesticated
It for us, materialised on preoccupied laps, and,
Mozart-addict, rushed in filthy-footed from
Uprooting lupins, to settle yourself round Primo's collar
When duets began.

Now the heir's installed, she colonises
The outposts (both next-doors, and one further)
Where she's feasted and fêted. Such cunning
Is natural to your prudent race, in case
Of catastrophe,

And I see, dear dead one, how we severed you
From your own earth, how you chose us to be
Your territory. You are there quite often,
Dear tabby blur, in my bad eye's corner. We left you
Nothing to haunt but ourselves.

Haunt us still, dear first-footer,
First to live with us, first to confirm
Us as livers-together, you who took us so simply
For granted, translator of life into
The vernacular of love.
You who saw love, where innocent others
Saw only convenience.

Amy Cook's Cottage

Three Poems for Amy Cook (1909-1998)

1. AMY SITS FOR HER PORTRAIT
   (for Peter and Victoria)

Like a pre-Cambrian hill, she looks down
Mildly at our callow landscape.
We stare, we ask. She endures, having learned
Over years to perform herself.

Her part is *racy rustic*; which she isn't.
Her standards are her own, so clearly better
She never explains them. We have to guess
Why she's brought her private shepherd's pie,

Solid among the pâtés and lasagne; why,
As we slop about in the sun, in shorts and sneakers,
She's upright in straw hat and floral print;
Why she takes posing seriously; why she sings,

Recites, talks about education; why the dogs
Revere her, lying in the shade behind her chair;
Why she never tells her age; why she's always saying
Rome wasn't built in a day. So old,

So many dead-end jobs, so clever, now
She lives in a different country, translates
Patiently into our language, knows how to tell her life
As if it were a story. She has the poise

Of one who never had a chance,
And yet is always listened to.
Not a *turn*, though that's how she plays it.

The speechless portrait speaks the truth.
Don't listen. Look.

2. AMY TELLS US

Why she brings her private shepherd's pie:

I d'like bacon. Don't like brown bread.
The chips was lovely. Piece of fish
I ad were cremated. I gave they
To the fowls.

Why she takes posing seriously:

I only ave to sit yur and
See the scenery. Whatever you want,
Love, don't be afraid to move it.
You can fiddle as much as you like.
There's sittens, and there's fidgets.
If e ain't right, say so.

Why she sings:

I d'know a few ditties.
Some o they modern songs be all right.

and recites:

'Behold, a giant am I!
Aloft here in my tower …'
(Moving her arms as they taught her at school.
Gets to the end, without flaw.)

and talks about education:

At school, they did teach we to remember.
When I did learn the alphabet, I did learn it

Frontards and backards. (And does it.)
Teachers wasn't afraid of kids in they days.
I did like Grimms' Tales. I know
Tis only imagination, but I did like en.
They did turn out good scholars in they days.

She won't tell her age. But she will tell you

I wasn't built in a day.

3. A TOUCH OF ECLAIR

A golden day for our dog when, passing that Coombe cottage,
She was given a chocolate eclair. Ever after,
Our dog appalled Long Street drivers, bounding over to Amy.

Old and straight like Westridge beeches,
We see her now in paintings, not as she was,
Waiting outside the Co-op with her shopping.

Swift and surprising, like the road from Nibley,
Her wit and her way with words. Gloucester
Has an archive; they study her vowels in Birmingham.

The endless bone-weary work she did on roads round Wotton
To clean them for us. Fish and chip paper,
Toffee papers, sweet papers, *all the ruddy lot*.

Something grand, something gold about Amy. Thin, old, poor,
She blessed us all with her blunt presence. A touch of eclair
At her funeral, when the Silver Band played her out.

Local Poet

Can't see so well now; his hearing
Isn't what it was. But he can still
Smell where a fox has been among the dahlias.

The birds have flown, the loft's empty,
But he still writes for *Pigeon Post*,
Plays cards with his ancient neighbour,

Works the garden. And suddenly,
A year ago, the Muse pounced:
He is her man in Gloucestershire.

The opposition doesn't worry him. *Betjeman, now –*
He rhymes too far apart. I have 'em close
Like church bells. I'm ready for publication.

Each poem's numbered like a show bird;
There's a prospectus: 'Purchasers will find them
Humorous, informative, historical.'

And so they will, they will. The W.I.
Like his stuff; and the Horticultural.
His voice helps. Double Gloucester,

Though it shouldn't be, he says. *I had the best*
Education available at that time.
But I liked to play with the wild boys,

And they spoke broad. Now he's the poet
For wild things, looks with a pigeon's eye
As far north as Evesham, tells how blackbirds

Lob home through ivy, where to find
The fishbone mixen of a kingfisher's nest,
Honours the useful stream by the elastic factory,

Explains how to direct hounds (*they know
Who Charlie is*), records shy Royalty's local earths,
The tragedy of the lame stray greyhound bitch

Whose litter the fox ate, gulls
Trailing wireworms down strict furrows,
Long-dead shires with hooves

As big as buckets, and remembers
Ol' Tucker Workman trapping the badger
Using his legs like tongs. But most of all

I like his garden ones, about the flowers
He grows but cannot spell, bees feverish
For marrow pollen, the evening mating call

Of woodlice, his iambic prescription
For limp cauliflowers of calomel dust
(*Obtainable from Boots*). How can I tell him

The competition judge won't pick his poems?
The Horticultural, the W. I. –
They ask him back, they think he's good,

And they know what he's on about. *This judge –
Where's he from, anyway? He won't know here.*
We settle which to send. He's disappointed

By what I like. I know he has no chance
Of winning. Does he trust me? No, I think.
Can he suspect I'll write about our talk,

And steal all his best lines? I hope he can't.
I hope he won't read this.

Pat at Milking Time

This enterprise is sick. The placid rats
Know it, roundhaunched and glossy, taking
Turns in the straw, like country dancers.

The dairy smells of defeat and sour milk.
Bank manager on Wednesday. Herb cheese
Drains peacefully through muslin into the churn.

The kids don't understand, knowing
Nothing but now, and the imperatives
Of suck, sleep, wriggle. In their world

It's normal to be fed at three o'clock
In the morning. What a field contains –
Sun, daisies, wind – is not to be imagined.

Growing up keeps them busy. But the milkers
Know, and are sad. They come to her pail
One by one, independently, as she calls them,

Christabel, Infanta, Treasure and Nickel,
Mosquito and *Gnat*, stepping thoughtfully,
Nibbling her straggly hair, weaving

Their sympathetic magic behind her back,
Watching through square-lensed eyes. Every day
There is less milk in their taut pronged teats.

Love is no help. Like cats they rub against her.
The church clock echoes oddly. The strident
Mew of a peacock slices the neutral air.

95

Three storeys up, she lives under the eaves
In the sky's suburbs. From above
She knows the tabby shoulders of pigeons,
The painted hair of men.

Downstairs is another country, its frontier
A childgate. On slippered, uncertain feet,
Armed with a Zimmer, she mans
The landing, her treacherous border.

Goliath voices intone in her
Diminishing kingdom, declaiming the weather's
Intentions, the future's enormous transactions.
Her armchair's horizon is global.

In it she waits for her tiny Doomsday.
Her drawers are tidied for good, and then
Untidied again. Life keeps on being picked up,
Like a tedious piece of knitting.

So she idles out her epilogue
In her eyrie, looking down upon living
As a small, difficult theorem
She could solve once. And in her windows

Her small, difficult plants turning sunwards
Obstinately, perpetually flower.

Strong Language in South Gloucestershire

Vocabulary of earth, names

Tough and diehard as crypts,
Cathedrals perched on their shoulders.

No committee okayed them.
They happened, like grass,

Written down all anyhow
By cosmopolitan clerks in a hurry.

Ramshackle riddles, their meaning
Deconstructed in aloof universities,

Their proper stresses a password
Known only to cautious locals.

Now, inscribed on steel, they confront drivers,
Looming on roads by the restriction signs,

Unreel their quirks along the prim
Mensuration of Ordnance Survey,

Still hard at it, still proclaiming
Here are Soppa's tinpot two acres,

Something holy, a good place for blackbirds,
Duck farm, bridge over mud,

The strangers' bright city.

(Various Sodburys; Nympsfield; Ozleworth; Doughton; Slimbridge;
Gloucester. These are all places in Gloucestershire.)

On Buying OS Sheet 163

I own all this. Not loutish acres
That tax the spirit, but the hawking
Eye's freehold, paper country.

Thirty-two inches of aqueduct,
Windmill (disused), club house, embankment,
Public conveniences

In rural areas. This my
Landlocked landscape that lives in cipher,
And is truer than walking.

Red and imperial, the Romans
Stride eastward. Mysterious, yellow,
The Salt Way halts and is gone.

Here, bigger than the hamlets they are,
Wild wayside syllables stand blooming:
Filkins, Lechlade, Broughton Poggs.

Here only I discard the umber
Reticulations of sad cities,
The pull and drag of mud.

Wotton on Valentine's Day

For OS 759934: 14.2.96. A Love-poem

She is my Corinna, my Lucasta,
Whose name, for courtesy, I will not say.

Like a tomboy, she sprawls among sharp small hills;
Like a sibyl, she drifts into silences and fog.

She has her own way with birds and flowers;
Is given to minor fierce festivals without much notice.

Her speech is like a mouthful of hot chestnuts.
Extra hs and ls give her vowels grace.

Her lovely highborn sisters over the hill
With their suitors and reputations look down on her.

She doesn't care, preferring her laidback cronies,
Symn, Bradley, Haw, Bear, Ragnall and Shinbone.

Her favourite scent: a dab of woodsmoke behind the ears.
Haute couture and haute cuisine are not her style.

She is an early riser, watery and echoing;
I love her then. And in the evening, when blackbirds call it a day.

In all the seasons of every year I love her.
And this seems as good a day as any to say so.

Approaching Wotton

Wotton Walks

These are old paths, designed
And kept alive by feet
For whom walking was
The only way of going.

These are treads of workers,
Plodding early with their bait
To quarries, mills, farms; haunts
Of fishermen; rides for fine
Ladies, cantering sidesaddle
Through polished woodland; sly poaching alleys;
Game-keepers' beats; loitering ways for children
Towards ball-games and arithmetic; paths
For dutiful daughters to mothers'
Picturesque rheumaticky cottages;
By-ways for primrose-finders; the straight gate
To church for tidy-suited hymn-singers;
Trails for dog-tired shepherds to remote
Huts at lamb-time; muddy channels
For heavy patient cows; close turf
And easy gravel for foxes and badgers
To travel after dark.
                              Enter this web
Spun by dead and living round Wotton.
Remember lovers keeping trysts
At special stiles, remember
Gipsies stealing down green lanes,
And the reflective fellows
Who watched and thought by bridges

Over small streams. Attend also
To the punctually returning
Tree, flower, bird, since what you see
Is as new as it's old.
                              Finally,
Come back satisfied, please, at peace,
To where Wotton pleats herself on her shelves
Above the vale, under the edge.

Conygre Wood and Hyakinthoides Non-Scriptus

(for Libby Houston)

This is how it is, here:
Native halflight. Rain off the Atlantic.
Rack of blue like sky growing
A foot above ground. Hush. Birdcalls.
Small puckered beech leaves, and earth,
Its muscle showing, hurdling up limestone,
With acres of blue on its back.

Disappointment to the early masters,
Dons, doctors, name-givers,
Like getting a girl when you wanted a boy.
They hoped for Hyakinthos, the beautiful,
Whose literate petals say *AI AI*
Sorry Sorry, inscribed by divine Apollo,
Who killed the lovely creature by mistake.

But our island gets this lot, illiterate
Non-scriptus flowers. Growing along with garlic,
Smelling of honey, careless of Latin snubs.
Blue and blue and blue and free
Of an invented grief, free
To come and go, to multiply, to chant
The noiseless bluebell anthem: *Here we are*.

Tyndale in Darkness

(for Michael Foot)

> Almost every good translation of the Bible ... has been
> undertaken by a single highly gifted zealot. Tyndale was
> executed before he could complete his task, but he set the
> English style ... which lives on in the King James Version
> (1611). A sacred book must be all of a piece, as though
> written by the hand of God Himself; and this can hardly
> happen unless a man of strong character, wide knowledge,
> and natural eloquence, working only for the love of God –
> perhaps under threat of death – sets his seal on it.

Robert Graves: *The Crane Bag*

> St Jerome also translated the Bible into his mother tongue:
> why may not we also?

William Tyndale

TUESDAY

Defecerunt sicut fumus dies mei et ossa sicut gremium aruerunt.
(My days are consumed like smoke, and my bones are burned as
an hearth)
(Ps 102:3)

The Old isn't as easy as the New.
Greek's nothing, but I needed Germany
To teach me Hebrew. Then the endless trail
That drags from Genesis to Malachi!
Now the New's finished, printed, launched on the world,
Doing its work in England, in plain English,
All clinched and Bristol fashion. But I
Not there to see it. Flushed out
From Gloucestershire first by a rout of clownish priests

42

Who, because they are unlearned, when they come together to the
ale-house, which is their preaching-place, they affirm that my
sayings are heresy.

Then in London, bluffed, swindled, bullied,
Hounded at last abroad.
                              Well, God's work
Can be done here too, though I miss the rough sweetness
Of English. But on the run always, always I need more time,
Space, books and peace to do things properly.
And light, and warmth. These I miss here
In my palatial jail, the Emperor's guest.
Still, I can get things done. But how I grieve
The watery deathbed of my Pentateuch
In the deep roadsteads off Holland. Back to the start
Again. I did them all again. All five.
But it held me back. Here I am now
Still toiling through the waste of Chronicles,
When I could be at the Psalms, dealing with hope,
Injury, loss, despair, treachery, joy,
Not endless histories, churned out by some
Dull priest with a long memory. Only five books to go
But how long have I? I get used to Death
Leaning over my shoulder, with his noose and brand,
Breathing at each sentence end. I know he waits his day,
But not the day itself. I doubt I'll ever reach
So far as the happy man who's like a tree
Planted by water, that brings forth his fruit in its season,
And look, whatsoever he doeth, it shall prosper.
Well, Miles gets the Psalms. My heir. He'll bring forth his fruit,
The happy man. But I too was planted by water,
Born with the tune of Gloucestershire in my head,
Knowing our English as much the language of heaven
As Jerome's tawdry Latin, pagan patter,
That Jesus and His fishers never spoke.

They say it cannot be translated into our tongue it is so rude. It is not so rude as they are false liars. For the Greek tongue agreeeth more with the English than with the Latin. And the properties of the Hebrew tongue agreeeth a thousand times more with the English than with the Latin.

Not many days left me, not many days.
They keep my working books, my Hebrew Bible,
Grammar and dictionary. I'd get on faster
If I had them, and light to work in the dark.
Sicut fumus dies mei, my days are consumed –
Consumed? An empty word. *Eaten* is better.
Defecerunt. Bloodless Latin! But English lives!
Will Miles be up to it? – yes, eaten
Like smoke, and smoke will finish me
Here, in the marketplace at Vilvorde. *Et ossa mea* –
And my bones burned up like a hearth.
That too. But here, while I live, in the cold and the dark,
I long for a whole shirt, and a lamp at night.

I suffer greatly from cold in the head, and am afflicted by a perpetual catarrh … My overcoat is worn out; my shirts are also worn out … And I ask to be allowed to have a lamp in the evening; it is indeed wearisome sitting alone in the dark.

WEDNESDAY

Vigilavi et factus sum sicut passer solitarius in tecto
(I watch, and am as a sparrow alone upon the house top)
(Ps 102:7)

He is the sparrow, the Friday lord.
I hoped to be the watcher on the rooftop,
But He was first. I'm flake of His fire,

Leaf-tip on His world-tree.
                                      But I watch too,
As once I stood on Nibley Knoll and looked
Out over moody Severn across the Forest
To the strangeness of Wales, Malvern's blue bony hills,
And down on the dear preoccupied people
Inching along to Gloucester, the trows with their sopping decks
Running from Bristol with the weather behind them,
And none of them knowing God's meaning, what He said to them,
Save filtered through bookish lips that never learnt
To splice a rope or fill a bucket. So I watched,
And saw the souls on the road, the souls on the river,
Were the ones Jesus loved. I saw that. Now I see
The landscape of my life,and how that seeing
Has brought me to this place, and what comes after.
So He saw the history of us, His people,
From Olivet. And told His men to watch.
*Vigilate ergo (nescitis enim quando dominus veniat; sero, an media
nocte, an gallo canto, an mane), ne cum venerit repente, inveniat
vos dormientes.**
They couldn't keep their eyes open, poor souls.
Vigilate. As well tell them to stand on their heads.
Erant enim oculi eorum gravati. For their eyes were heavy.
I doubt I'd have done much better.
It must have been a hard day for them,
And they weren't used to late nights, the disciples,
But to early mornings, when the shoals come in.
Hard-headed men with blisters on their palms
From the nets. Why did He ask them to stay awake
When He knew they couldn't? Because He always does.
He picks the amateurs who follow Him
For love, not devout professionals
With a safe pair of hands. Look at Peter,
A man permanently in hot water, chosen,
Perhaps, for that very thing. God sets His mark
On us all. You start, and it's easy:

I heard the ploughboy whistling under Coombe Hill,
And I thought, *I could do that*. Give him God's word,
I mean, in his own workaday words. And I did,
But it got so difficult: exile, hardship, shipwreck,
Spies everywhere. Then prison, and the fire.
God's mark on me, as on Peter. I would have slept, too.

THURSDAY

Principes persecuti sunt me gratis.
(Princes have persecuted me without a cause)
(Ps 119:161)

What can you do with power except misuse it?
Being so mighty makes these men afraid
That we, their subjects, might guess they're men too.
That I can understand. It's the followers
Who turn my stomach. The glib climbers
Greedy for money, land, influence, jobs for the boys.
They're drawn by the power and the glory,
And kings aren't fastidious. Consider Henry's men –
Cuthbert the cloth-eared Bishop of London;
Wolsey the Suffolk wolf; and foul-mouthed More,
The bitterest tongue in England. Consider also
Their noble master Henry, the subject-harrier,
Who drove me here. Well then, consider them.
They fear me. So they should. I plan
The invasion of England by the word of God.
And it will come. Just now, they burn my books.
An easy step from that to burning clerks,
Burning this clerk for doing what God wants,
Turning God's word to King's English.

But not the King's;

---

* Watch ye therefore, for ye know not when the master of the house cometh, at even, or at
midnight, or at the cockcrowing, or in the morning: lest coming suddenly he find you
sleeping.

46

The people's; England's English. That's where Christ is.
Not a king to do business with Popes and chancellors,
But a servant, a man beneath us, who washes our feet,
Who goes before to try out the hard things first,
Who opens gates so we can go easily through,
That is the king, one and only, who speaks our own words.
The powerlessness and the glory.

Princes have persecuted me. Perhaps they have a cause.

FRIDAY

Scribantur haec in generationem alteram et populus qui creabitur laudabit
Dominum.
(This shall be written for those that come after: and the people which shall
be born shall praise the Lord)
(Ps 102:18)

The powerlessness. This is the day He dies,
Jesus, the Friday sparrow, the watcher on the cross
Who forgives those who put Him there. He's dying now,
And His world is dying too. I made this world twice
After God; twice I translated Genesis. I know
The deep places in it. And God said,
Let there be light, and there was light.
The accurate voice of God. And after him, me;
Tyndale of Nibley. The human small-scale words
For the unimagined thing. And as Jesus hangs dying,
That same immense familiar light, that shines
Over Nibley and Bristol, London and Flanders,
Over all the countries we know glancingly of,
Goes out, as the world, more faithful than its people,
Mourns for its maker. The world itself dies.

God says, Let there be no light.
And when the sixth hour was come, there was darkness over the
                    whole land until the ninth hour.

47

Starlings think it night, celandines shut their petals,
Trees in Westridge Wood stand frostily waiting.
No light. No light. God said let there be no light,
While Jesus is dying.
                              I want to die like that,
Brave and forgiving. I may not be able.
The grace is not in us. We have to ask.

We must also desire God day and night instantly to open our eyes.

So little time. We have to hustle God
Who, in His unhorizoned sphere of time,
Can hardly know how short our seasons are.
And I pray too for resurrection in the word.
This shall be written for those who come after.
And still, these tedious Chronicles waiting for me,
These kings and priests and rulers of this world,
These Jeroboams and Jehoiakims,
Between me and *beatus vir*, the happy man,
Whose leaf shall not wither. Unlike mine.
And look, whatsoever he doeth it shall prosper.
Et omnia quaecumque faciet prosperabuntur.
Prosperabuntur? God's teeth, what a word
For Christian tongues to wrestle with. Language for liars!
Our dear and patient English shall rip out
The rubbish Jerome stuffed in the Church's mouth.
I must get on. Day and night. Instantly.
The Psalms are waiting. So are the English.
Vile the place is, but still my Father's house.
Lampless or not, He lights it.

Notes to *Tyndale in Darkness*

Who, because … are heresy: Tyndale, quoted in Demaus, *William Tindale*, London, 1886.

The Emperor: Charles V.

My Pentateuch: Tyndale's first translation of this was lost when his boat sank.

The happy man: Psalm 1.i: 'Blessed is the man that walketh not in the counsel of the ungodly … he shall be like a tree planted by the rivers of water.'

Miles: Miles Coverdale, who worked with Tyndale and took over at his death. *The Book of Common Prayer* Psalms are Coverdale's.

Jerome: translated the Old and New Testaments from Hebrew and Greek into Latin (the Vulgate).

They say … with the Latin: from Tyndale's *The Obedience of a Christian Man*.

Vilvorde: where, in 1536, Tyndale was strangled and burned.

I suffer … in the dark: letter from Tyndale, imprisoned in Vilvorde Castle.

Nibley Knoll: in Gloucestershire, where the Tyndale Monument now stands.

Trows: Severn barges.

Vigilate ergo … dormientes: Matthew 24.42.

Erant … gravati: Matthew 26.43.

Cuthbert: Cuthbert Tunstall, Bishop of London.

More: Sir Thomas More was more vituperative in polemic even than Tyndale – which is saying something!

Twice … Genesis: the first translation was lost in the Rhine shipwreck.

And when … ninth hour: Mark 15.33.

Westridge Wood: on the ridge above North Nibley.

We must also … our eyes: from Tyndale's *A Prologue*.

49

Dear Mr Lee

Dear Mr Lee (Mr Smart says
it's rude to call you Laurie, but that's
how I think of you, having lived with you
really all year), Dear Mr Lee
(Laurie) I just want you to know
I used to hate English, and Mr Smart
is roughly my least favourite person,
and as for Shakespeare (we're doing him too)
I think he's a national disaster, with all those jokes
that Mr Smart has to explain why they're jokes,
and even then no one thinks they're funny,
and T. Hughes and P. Larkin and that lot
in our anthology, not exactly a laugh a minute,
pretty gloomy really, so that's why
I wanted to say Dear Laurie (sorry) your book's
the one that made up for the others, if you
could see my copy you'd know it's lived
with me, stained with Coke and Kitkat
and when I had a cold, and I often
take you to bed with me to cheer me up
so Dear Laurie, I want to say sorry,
I didn't want to write a character-sketch
of your mother under headings, it seemed
wrong somehow when you'd made her so lovely,
and I didn't much like those questions
about *social welfare in the rural community*
and *the seasons as perceived by an adolescent*,
I didn't think you'd want your book
read that way, but bits of it I know by heart,
and I wish I had your uncles and your half-sisters
and lived in Slad, though Mr Smart says your view
of the class struggle is naïve, and the examiners
won't be impressed by me knowing so much by heart,

they'll be looking for terse and cogent answers
to their questions, but I'm not much good at terse and cogent,
I'd just like to be like you, not mind about being poor,
see everything bright and strange, the way you do,
and I've got the next one out of the Public Library,
about Spain, and I asked Mum about learning
to play the fiddle, but Mr Smart says Spain isn't
like that any more, it's all Timeshare villas
and Torremolinos, and how old were you
when you became a poet? (Mr Smart says for anyone
with my punctuation to consider poetry as a career
is enough to make the angels weep.)

PS   Dear Laurie, please don't feel guilty for
me failing the exam, it wasn't your fault,
it was mine, and Shakespeare's,
and maybe Mr Smart's, I still love *Cider*,
it hasn't made any difference.

Staff Party

Silky and bland, like Roman emperors,
With kiss-curls trained across their noble brows,
They sit, my colleagues, laughing in the right
Self-conscious way at all the proper points.

I've known them for so long, and yet I don't
Know them at all. I know their parlour tricks,
Their favourite cardigans and recipes,
Their hairdressers, their views about the split
Infinitive, the Principal and What
Is Wrong with Modern Parents, know the names
Of children, husbands, cats. I know that when
Some local battle clouds relationships
(Shoplifting, drugs, the press or pregnancy –
So many trivial things can go astray
Besides the bigger, permanent mishaps:
The timetable, or the supply of ink),
Some will orate, some help, and some betray.

We know what each will do. But some cold hand
Stops us from knowing more. That's dangerous,
Even disloyal. For already we
Know more than's proper about all of us.

We know our reputations and nicknames,
Enthusiast, digressor, confidante,
The one who just can't concentrate on girls
Because she's getting married, and the one
Who never does her washing. Emperors
Preserved their Roman calm in public life,
Unless they liked it otherwise, but these
Statuesque Romans have Suetonius

Around them all the time, scribbling on desks,
Asking discursive questions, argus-eyed,
Flypaper-memoried historians,
Publishing every moment of the day
Sober surmises and fantastic truth.

Knowing all this, and knowing we are known,
We must respect the anonymity
We decent ladies all pretend to have,
Letting the Whore, the Genius, the Witch,
The Slut, the Miser and the Psychopath
Go down to history, if they really must,
While Caesar keeps his bright precarious gloss.

Carol Concert

Before the ice has time to form
On the carparked windscreens, before
A single carol has announced itself,
The performance happens.
(sing lullaby virgin noel)

These sculptured hairdos, these fairy-
Tale dresses, gothic embraces –
Sophie, long time no see! – are they
The approved offering
(sing lullaby virgin noel)

To the dull obligatory
Young men, whose correct accent, tie
And sex are paraded like expensive
Perfume? Or is it friends
(sing lullaby virgin noel)

Who get this oblation? Known once
Sweaty, tearful, giggling, asleep,
In the undesigning equality
Of youth, now moving high
(sing lullaby virgin noel)

Into the difficult heavens
Of Hotel Management in Kent,
Of sitting Oxbridge, of getting married?
In the carpark ice forms,
(sing lullaby virgin noel)

In the hall inarticulate
Strange friendships falter. *The standard*
Of singing (they say) *has gone down. They must*
Be missing us. Prefects
(sing lullaby virgin noel)

Like angels watch with wondering eyes.
Next year perhaps they too will sport
Long curtain fabric skirts and Afro hair,
But their present faces
(sing lullaby virgin noel)

Deny complicity. The young
Bored man says he's having a ball,
While the choir with the innocent mouths
Of singers cry
Lullaby, virgin, noel.

Last House

Like the dead march, the beat of destruction is slow.
The crane-man stirs; the giant ball moves over;
A hum; a waver; a trickle of mortar; a pause;
A slice of wall flops over out of the sun.

This is the last performance. The Regal yaws doubtfully
As audiences do, wanting the star to fall,
But not till the last reel, at sunset, to the right music.

The crowd remembers whistling in limelit smoke,
Organist rising astride his yodelling nag,
Usherettes with torches and no-nonsense style,
Chocolates, cigarettes, trayclad girl in a spotlight,

Buckled backseat couples, gauging how far they can go,
Persistent men in macs at matinees,
Lustrous magnified eyes oozing slow motion tears,
Hi-ho-ing dwarfs, hi-yo-ing cowboys, Hitchcock.

Here once they studied poker-faced dialogue
(Here's lookin' at ya, kid); here they learnt
How to sing in the rain; to hamlet; to tootsie; to catch 22;
How to make passionate love to Elizabeth Taylor.

Where now the oilfields of ketchup, the acres of hair?
A shame to knock the old place down, they say,
Drifting along, *We had some good times here*.

Celluloid shades of Garbo, Garland, Groucho,
Welles, Goofy, Wayne, rise hissing in the air,
And *Hi-yo!* the call sounds high and very far off,
Let's go, big fella! Hi-yo, Silver, away!

What about Jerusalem?

Wallflowers in your garden are stubbornly rooted,
Heeled in by you.Your magnolia sprouts fierce black buds.

In Sheffield and Gloucestershire, babies you drew into light
Flower and grow upright. A knack of giving life.

(*I know them all*, you'd swagger. *At least, their mothers I do*.)
They won't forget you, pain-killer, comforter.

Now you lie here in the chapel in pale wood,
White and yellow mortal flowers, and we sing

Jerusalem tentatively, waiting for you to pop up and exclaim
You've left out the feeling. So we have. I don't want to feel,

Gwen, that you've ended anything. *I will not cease*, we drone.
We haven't even started in the Great-heart way you did,

Who challenged geriatric consultants, hauled your friend
Out of dementia, brought her home to live.

Dear Gwen, who made the worst coffee I've ever tried
Not to drink, who never remembered a name

(*You I mean! Whatnot!*), who told explicit obstetric stories
Loudly, embarrassingly, in public rooms,

Who loved fast cars (*they pull in the birds*)
To my priggish disapproval; whose driving was known to the
police.

I argued more with you than with anyone ever,
Though I'd seen you wink as you started to wind me up.

Is this all? Has that relentlessly
Self-educated mind at last run out of steam?

And such a little coffin. There's some trick here.
What about Jerusalem? You haven't ceased, have you?

The Coates Portal, (the east end of the Sapperton Tunnel, Thames & Severn Canal)

Canal 1977

I remember this place: the conspiratorial
Presence of trees, the leaves' design
On uncommitted water, the pocky stonework
Ruining mildly in mottled silence,
The gutted pub, the dropping sounds
Inside the tunnel. I remember this place.

And before. I remember the sly lurchers,
The rose-and-castled barges, serious horses,
Coal smell, the leggers' hollow whoops
Down water, the bankrupt contractors
Grizzling into their beer, the trees and grass
Waiting to take over. I remember before.

And I remember the not-yet after,
When the money's raised and the sparetime Sunday
Navvying's over, the last intrusive sapling
Is ashes, when the bunting has bobbed, the first
Distinguished head ducked under the keystone,
There will be an after to be remembered

As the pleasurecraft purr their idle way
Into sunshine, and the smooth pink families
With their superior dogs enjoy the water,
The weather, the picturesque antiquity
That savaged so many who made it.
I remember after. And after

And before, the mute persistence of water
And grass and trees. Humanity goes out
Like a light, like the Roman-candle miners,
Shafting their pits on a donkey-winch, astraddle
A powderkeg, light in their teeth, a fuse in each pocket,
Lying foreign and broken in Gloucestershire churchyards now.

Narrow Boat TINKER

Purton Lower Bridge

Affable water lips and chats
Along iron-bound banks. A cruiscr's wakc
Wags unendingly after it, floats flouncing
Like cross dowagers with long memories.
Not many boats in autumn. Boys
Lend a hand with ropes, show their catch
(A dead eel). The low swung bridge
Opens when needed, smoothly, like a sliced smile.

This is the human scale: nothing too much.
But half a mile downstream sprawls Glumdalclitch,
Naked, enormous, careless, bright with mud,
Red sun squat on her, pocked by birdfeet, cables,
Monstrously tidal, impossible, uncivil,
Desirable, the lethal river Severn.

The Invitation

The Gloucestershire foxes' message
To the child beyond the sea:
We d'hear thee was born in a stable.
Us dreams uneasy of thee.

Us knows the pack be after thee,
Us knows how that du end,
The chase, the kill, the cheering,
Dying wi'out a friend.

So lover, us makes this suggestion
To thee and thy family tu:
Come live wi we under Westridge
Where the huntin folk be few.

Thee'll play wi cubs in the sunshine,
Sleep in our snuggest den,
And feed on – well, us'll see to that –
Forget they beastly men.

Maybe thee thinks tis too far off,
Our language strange to thee,
But remember us foxes of Westridge
When thou tires of humanity.

The Wicked Fairy at the Manger

My gift for the child:

No wife, kids, home;
No money sense. Unemployable.
Friends, yes. But the wrong sort –
The workshy, women, wogs,
Petty infringers of the law, persons
With notifiable diseases,
Poll tax collectors, tarts,
The bottom rung.
     His end?
I think we'll make it
Public, prolonged, painful.

Right, said the baby. *That was roughly
What we had in mind.*

The Apple War

The storm troops have landed,
The red and the green,
Their pips on their shoulders,
Their skin brilliantine.

Uniform, orderly,
Saleable, ambitious –
Gala and Granny
And Golden Delicious.

Quarter them, they're tasteless;
They've cottonwool juice,
But battalions of thousands
Routinely seduce.

In shy hen-haunted orchards
Twigs faintly drum,
Patient as partisans
Whose time has almost come,

From Worcester and Somerset,
Sussex and Kent,
They'll ramble singing,
A fruity regiment.

Down with Cinderella's kind,
Perfect, toxic, scarlet;
Back comes the old guard,
Costard, Crispin, Russet,

James Grieve, Ashmead's Kernel,
Coppin, Kingston Black –
Someone has protected them.

They're coming back.

Awkward Subject

The light is wonderful, he says. Not light
For house-agents, certainly. They avoid
November shots, when wisped and bony trees
Throw a disturbing shade on property.

Stand there. Just a bit further. Don't look at the dog.
My casual adaptation to the place
(One hand in pocket, right knee slightly bent)
May not be what I mean, but is in danger
Of immortality.

                I feel my teeth support me
Against my inner lip; face him with all my skin.
Sensing my misery, *Would you rather smile?*
He asks. And break the lens, I hope. Words are my element.
Photograph them.

Kitchen sink, with fruitbowl

Earthed

Not precisely, like a pylon or
A pop-up toaster, but in a general
Way, stuck in the mud.

Not budding out of it like gipsies,
Laundry lashed to a signpost, dieting on
Nettles and hedgehogs,

Not lodged in its layers like badgers,
Tuned to the runes of its home-made walls, wearing
Its shape like a skin,

Not even securely rooted, like
Tribesmen tied to the same allotment, sure of
The local buses,

But earthed for all that, in the chalky
Kent mud, thin sharp ridges between wheel-tracks, in
Surrey's wild gravel,

In serious Cotswold uplands, where
Limestone confines the verges like yellow teeth,
And trees look sideways.

Everything from the clouds downwards holds
Me in its web, like the local newspapers,
Routinely special,

Or Somerset belfries, so highly
Parochial that Gloucestershire has none, or
Literate thrushes,

Conscientiously practising the
Phrases Browning liked, the attitude Hughes noticed,
Or supermarkets

Where the cashiers' rudeness is native
To the district, though the bread's not, or gardens,
Loved more than children,

Bright with resourcefulness and smelling
Of rain. This narrow island charged with echoes
And whispers snares me.